AMERICAN SPACE MISSIONS
ASTRONAUTS, EXPLORATION, AND DISCOVERY

Space Shuttle Disaster
The Tragic Mission of the Challenger

Henry M. Holden

Enslow Publishers, Inc.
40 Industrial Road
Box 398
Berkeley Heights, NJ 07922
USA

http://www.enslow.com

Original edition published as *The Tragedy of the Space Shuttle* Challenger in 2004.

Library of Congress Cataloging-in-Publication Data
Holden, Henry M.
  Space shuttle disaster : the tragic mission of the challenger / Henry M. Holden.
      p. cm.
  "Original edition published as The Tragedy of the Space Shuttle Challenger in 2004"—T.p. verso.
  Includes bibliographical references and index.
    ISBN 978-0-7660-4073-1
  1. Challenger (Spacecraft)—Accidents—Juvenile literature. 2. Space shuttles—Accidents—Juvenile literature. I. Holden,
Henry M. Tragedy of the Space Shuttle Challenger. II. Title.
  TL867.H649 2013
  363.12'4—dc23
                                    2011044934
Future editions:
Paperback ISBN 978-1-4644-0078-0
ePUB ISBN 978-1-4645-0985-8
PDF ISBN 978-1-4646-0985-5

Printed in the United States of America
032012 Lake Book Manufacturing, Inc., Melrose Park, IL
10 9 8 7 6 5 4 3 2 1

To Our Readers: We have done our best to make sure all Internet addresses in this book were active and appropriate when we went to press. However, the author and the publisher have no control over and assume no liability for the material available on those Internet sites or on other Web sites they may link to. Any comments or suggestions can be sent by e-mail to comments@enslow.com or to the address on the back cover.

♻ Enslow Publishers, Inc., is committed to printing our books on recycled paper. The paper in every book contains 10% to 30% post-consumer waste (PCW). The cover board on the outside of each book contains 100% PCW. Our goal is to do our part to help young people and the environment too!

Illustration Credits: AP Images, p. 15; AP Images / Bob Daugherty, p. 32; AP Images / Bruce Weaver, p. 7; AP Images / Dave Einsel, p. 41; AP Images / Haraz N. Ghanbari, p. 37; AP Images / NASA, p. 30; NASA Johnson Space Center, pp. 13, 17, 24, 26, 34; NASA Kennedy Space Center, pp. 1, 4, 8, 20, 23, 29, 38; NASA Marshall Space Flight Center, p. 10.

Cover Illustration: NASA Kennedy Space Center (The space shuttle *Challenger* launch on January 28, 1986).

Contents

CHAPTER 1

The Final Voyage

It was early Tuesday morning, January 28, 1986. The weather at Cape Canaveral was frigid. The night before, the temperature had gone below freezing. People could see icicles on the launchpad. The Florida sun was warming the air and would soon begin to melt the two-foot icicles. It was the coldest day ever for a space shuttle launch.

This launch had captured worldwide attention. It was going to carry Sharon Christa McAuliffe, a history teacher, into space.[1] She was going to be the first passenger/observer of the Teacher in Space Program.

There were concerns in the Mission Control Center. They had asked for three ice inspections of the rockets and the shuttle *Challenger*. The third inspection, shortly before launch, showed the ice had melted onto the launchpad. The flight had been postponed six times due to bad weather and mechanical issues. There had been another two-hour delay earlier in the morning. A part in the launch processing system had failed during fueling.

At T-(for takeoff) minus six seconds, *Challenger*'s main engines fired. Huge billowing columns of flame and smoke surrounded the base of the shuttle. Within four seconds, the engines were burning at 90 percent power.

The launch is the most dangerous part of the flight. The external fuel tank was filled with 528,600 gallons (more than 2 million liters) of explosive fuel. They help generate 2.6 million pounds (1.7 million kilograms) of thrust.

At T-minus zero seconds, the two white solid fuel rocket boosters ignited. These were attached to each side of the huge external fuel tank. Each of the boosters carried more than 1.1 million pounds (498,952 kilograms) of solid fuel. They were to help the main engines lift the shuttle to a speed of 3,512 miles per hour (5,652 kilometers per hour). The shuttle roared off the pad and into the sky. Five miles (8 kilometers) away, hundreds of spectators could feel the ground shaking beneath their feet.[2]

Liftoff

Liftoff occurred at 11:38 A.M. The rockets boosted the shuttle off the launchpad. *Challenger* arched up through the air, leaving a thick trail of smoke behind. This was *Challenger*'s tenth mission. McAuliffe and the crew, commander Francis "Dick" Scobee, pilot Michael J. Smith, and mission specialists Judith A. Resnik, Ellison S. Onizuka, Ronald E. McNair, and Gregory B. Jarvis, awaited the upcoming mission.

For the first sixty seconds, all systems seemed to work perfectly. At T-plus seventy seconds, Mission Control told Commander Scobee to "throttle up." This means the pilot increases the speed of the shuttle. Three seconds later, Smith said, "uhh . . . oh!"[3] Then all communications ended.[4]

Spectators watch the space shuttle *Challenger* lift off from Kennedy Space Center on January 28, 1986. After the first sixty seconds of the launch, all systems seemed to work well.

Millions of people around the world watched the *Challenger* explode just seventy-two seconds into the launch. This photo, taken a few seconds after the accident, shows exhaust plumes from the shuttle's main engines and the solid rocket booster entwined around a ball of gas from the external fuel tank.

Millions of people were watching on television. Due to the fact that McAullife was on board, thousands of schoolchildren were part of this audience. They were following the thick white vapor trail behind the shuttle. At 58.8 seconds into the flight, a flame, later seen on enhanced film, was coming from the right solid rocket booster. At 72 seconds, there was a sudden chain of events that destroyed *Challenger* and the seven crew members on board. All these events happened in less than two seconds. A huge white cloud formed where the shuttle had been. From within the white cloud came a horrific flaming ball of fire.

Moments before, people had been filled with joy. Now no one could believe what he or she had just seen. The rocket had blown to pieces. It was the worst tragedy in the history of the space program.

Perhaps not until the attack on the World Trade Center towers, on September 11, 2001, did American children and adults have such a terrible feeling inside as they did when they watched the destruction of *Challenger*. Sadly, this would not be the last time the world would watch a space shuttle tragedy. On February 1, 2003, the shuttle *Columbia* broke apart on reentry into Earth's atmosphere.

The space shuttle *Challenger* in Earth orbit in 1983. This was the second space shuttle that NASA built, and it joined the fleet in 1982.

CHAPTER 2

Launch Background

Challenger **was the name** of the orbiter that was to carry the astronauts into space. It was attached to a large orange external fuel tank and two solid rocket boosters. It was the second shuttle built, and it had joined the National Aeronautics and Space Administration (NASA) fleet in 1982. It was named for a ship that explored uncharted ocean waters a century earlier.

Launch Delays

Challenger STS (flight) 51–L was scheduled to launch in July 1985. However, by the time the crew was assigned, the launch had been postponed to November. The *Challenger* launch was now behind schedule. *Challenger* was finally rescheduled for launch in late January. The pressure was on NASA. Additional delays would have a negative effect on the coming shuttle launches. They, too, would have to be postponed.

On Monday, January 27, the Florida temperatures began to drop. At night, they dipped to 24°F (–4°C) at the launch site. The wind chill factor made it feel as if it were –10°F (–23°C).[1] At dawn, the temperature began to rise slowly. Engineers from the company that built the solid fuel rocket boosters were very worried. They had experience with launches in cold weather. It could be dangerous to the astronauts. On earlier flights, some rubber seals, called O-rings, within the solid rocket boosters suffered damage from superheated gases. The damage had occurred at launch temperatures much higher than on this day. Up to that time, the lowest launch temperature had been 53°F (11.7°C). However, because the engineers could not show positive proof that the launch could be dangerous, NASA decided to launch *Challenger* anyway.

The NASA television cameras showed the astronauts shivering in the icy wind. They walked carefully along the giant steel-framed gantry, two hundred feet above the launchpad. They did not want to slip and fall on the ice.[2]

As the sun rose, it revealed a clear blue, cloudless sky. It looked like a perfect day to fly. However, it was still too cold. It was about 28°F (–2.2°C), and there was ice on the launchpad.[3] At T-minus nine minutes, there was a routine ten-minute hold. NASA would extend this hold until the temperature rose to 36°F (2.2°C).[4]

By 11:00 A.M., four hours later, the sun had warmed the outside of the launch vehicle. Everyone expected the countdown to resume. Twenty minutes before liftoff, the ice team made another inspection.

Icicles are visible on the launchpad and service tower before the *Challenger* was scheduled to launch on January 28, 1986. Frigid temperatures and ice delayed the launch for several hours.

An engineer watching on closed-circuit television from California called the Cape. He asked NASA to delay the launch again.[5] The warm sun on the outside would not solve the problem that worried him. Without the direct rays of the sun, the rubber O-rings would stay cold and brittle. The more brittle the O-rings, the greater the chance they would fail.

NASA resumed the countdown, and *Challenger* lifted off. It was the twenty-fifth shuttle mission in less than five years. Many thought these flights were now routine and that all the danger had been eliminated.

Rocket Ignition

When the solid rocket boosters fired, a puff of black smoke came from the lower joint of the right booster rocket. At the time, no one noticed the black smoke because it mixed in with the regular ignition smoke. Almost as quickly as it appeared, it was gone.

Engine failure during launch would call for a "RTLS"—Return To Launch Site.[6] The pilot could fire bolts that would release the orbiter from the fuel tank and boosters.[7] *Challenger* would then land at the Kennedy Space Center or another landing spot. The earliest point this could happen would be after the solid rocket boosters had burned out and dropped off. This would be about two and a half minutes into the launch.[8] The shuttle could not physically separate while the solid rocket boosters were thrusting.[9] As a result, there would be no escape for the *Challenger* astronauts. On this launch, there was no warning of a malfunction. Seventy-three seconds into the launch, *Challenger* exploded. It had been traveling at almost twice the speed of sound when the explosion tore it to pieces.[10] It did not look like anyone could have survived the horrific blast. The crew cabin, forming the nose of *Challenger*, made it through the blast intact. For a few moments, it continued upward, to an altitude of 65,000 feet (19,812 meters).[11] It then fell toward the ocean below. The disaster was the worst for NASA since the first *Apollo* moon capsule burned on its launchpad in 1967, killing three astronauts.

Shock and Disbelief

The accident became one of the most significant events of the 1980s. Millions around the world watched it on live television. A moment earlier, the students at Christa McAuliffe's Concord, New Hampshire, high school were cheering the launch. Her parents, Ed and Grace

Two spectators react at the Kennedy Space Center after witnessing the *Challenger* space shuttle explosion. Millions of people watched the tragedy live, including Christa McAuliffe's students at her Concord, New Hampshire, high school.

Corrigan, had flown to the Cape with eighteen third-graders to watch the launch.[12] They all stared in disbelief. McAuliffe's husband, Steven, her son, Scott, and daughter, Caroline, sat in McAuliffe's dormitory room in shock.

Jane Smith, wife of pilot Mike Smith, knew something terrible had happened. "They're gone," she said. Her son asked, "What do you mean, Mom?" "They're lost," was all she could say.[13] One of Mike Smith's children cried out, "Daddy! Daddy! I want you. Daddy!

You promised nothing would happen."[14] Later, Cheryl Moore McNair told her children, "We won't be able to see Daddy anymore, physically, but we would be able to feel him, spiritually."[15]

For thirty seconds, the loudspeakers at the launch site were silent. By then, everyone realized the cloud of smoke from the rockets was no longer rising. Then, over the loudspeakers, came a voice from Mission Control: "Flight controllers are looking very carefully at the situation. Obviously a major malfunction. We have no downlink." This meant there were no data or radio signals coming from the shuttle. Then, what many had suspected was confirmed. "We have a report . . . that the vehicle has exploded."[16]

Immediately after the explosion, the astronaut's families were put in buses and rushed to the crew's quarters. NASA wanted to get them away from the reporters. There would be too many questions and no answers, yet.

Crew Recovery

It took about an hour for the debris to stop raining down from the sky. Then, NASA began a search-and-rescue effort for survivors although no one actually believed that anyone could have survived the explosion. Late that afternoon, NASA announced there were no signs that the crew had survived.

In Washington, D.C., President Ronald Reagan was going to give his State of the Union speech that evening. However, when he heard about the accident, he canceled his speech. Instead, he used the time to talk

A work crew lowers wreckage from the *Challenger* explosion into an abandoned missile silo at Cape Canaveral Air Force Station. Search-and-rescue teams covered 1,200 square miles of ocean looking for debris from the space shuttle.

to the nation. "The future does not belong to the fainthearted; it belongs to the brave," he said. "The *Challenger* crew was pulling us into the future, and we'll continue to follow them."[17]

Dozens of ships and aircraft searched for debris. The search covered about 1,200 square miles (3,108 square kilometers) of ocean. The ships used electronic devices, such as sonar, to look for pieces of wreckage. Mini-submarines searched for the astronauts. Some of the wreckage was more than 1,000 feet (304.8 meters) deep. All floating debris and any underwater debris considered important would be collected and brought ashore.

On March 9, recovery teams found the crew cabin in 100 feet (30.5 meters) of water. The bodies of the astronauts were inside, still strapped in their seats. Scientists studied the wreckage in an attempt to determine what killed the crew. The crew compartment was hardened and found separate from the shuttle cargo bay. However, the crash of the crew compartment into the ocean was violent. The force of the impact was far more than the human body could withstand.[18]

NASA could not positively determine what had killed the astronauts. It was possible they said, but not certain, that the crew lost consciousness in the seconds following the explosion. At an altitude of 45,000 feet (13,716 meters), when the explosion took place, loss of cabin pressure would have caused rapid loss of consciousness. The explosion stopped the flow of oxygen to the crew. Each crew member had a personal air pack with an emergency oxygen supply. These must be turned on by hand. Searchers found four air packs. Three of them had been turned on.[19] More than half the air in these packs had been used. Some of the crew may have lived long enough to activate their emergency air supplies. It took about two and a half minutes for the crew compartment to fall to the ocean. It fell at about 200 miles per hour (321.9 kilometers per hour). The impact with the ocean had probably caused their deaths. By then, all of the crew members were most likely unconscious.[20]

CHAPTER 3

The Seven Heroes

There are three types of astronauts on a typical shuttle flight: the flight crew, mission specialists, and payload specialists. They each have specific jobs.

The *Challenger* crew was an example of diversity at its best. They mirrored the American population in terms of race, gender, and religion. Among the seven heroes was an African American, Caucasian Americans, and an Asian American. There were women, Christians, a Jew, and a Buddhist.

Flight Crew

The flight crew consists of the shuttle commander and the pilot. The commander is in charge of the shuttle and the crew and is responsible for the mission's success and safety. The forty-six-year-old spacecraft commander, Francis R. Scobee, was a former air force mechanic. He had gone to night school and earned a college degree in engineering. This qualified him to become an officer and a pilot. He served in the Vietnam War and later became an air force test pilot. Scobee flew more

The *Challenger* crew poses for a photo following the end of the Terminal Countdown Demonstration Test, which simulates the final hours of a launch countdown. In this photo, from left to right, are Christa McAuliffe, Gregory Jarvis, Judy Resnik, Dick Scobee, Ronald McNair, Michael Smith, and Ellison Onizuka.

than forty-five types of aircraft, logging more than 6,500 hours of flight time. He and his wife, June, had two children.

Scobee was the pilot on the fifth flight of *Challenger* in April 1984. During this mission, the crew successfully repaired a broken satellite. This was an important mission. It showed that a shuttle crew could repair satellites in orbit. Scobee loved his job. He once said, "You know, it's a real crime to be paid for a job that I have so much fun doing."[1]

The pilot for mission 51–L was forty-year-old Captain Michael J. Smith. He was married to Jane Jarrell, and they had three children.

Smith flew A–6 Intruders during the Vietnam War. Later, he worked as a test pilot for the navy, flying twenty-eight different aircraft. This was his first spaceflight.

Mission Specialists

Mission specialists operate the mechanical systems on the shuttle. They may launch satellites and sometimes make spacewalks. Ellison S. Onizuka was thirty-nine years old and a lieutenant colonel in the air force. He and his wife, Lorna, had two children. He was born in Hawaii to parents of Japanese-American descent. Before becoming an astronaut, he was a U.S. Air Force test pilot. He was the first Asian American in space when he climbed aboard the *Discovery* in 1985. This *Challenger* mission was his second spaceflight.

Thirty-six-year-old Judith A. Resnik had a doctorate degree in electrical engineering. She enjoyed playing classical piano. Resnik joined NASA with the first group of female astronauts in 1978. In 1983, Sally Ride became the first American woman in space on board *Challenger*. Resnik became the second woman in space on board *Discovery* a year later. The dangers of spaceflight did not worry her. "I think something is only dangerous if you are not prepared for it," she said, "or if you don't have control over it or if you can't think through how to get yourself out of a problem."[2]

Ronald E. McNair was thirty-five years old and married to an educator, Cheryl Moore McNair. They had two children. McNair, born in South Carolina, attended the segregated public schools of the day.

He studied hard and was the valedictorian of his high school class. McNair went on to attend the Massachusetts Institute of Technology, where he specialized in laser physics and earned a doctorate degree. He once told a group of students, "The true courage of spaceflight is not sitting aboard 6 million pounds of fire and thunder as one rockets away from this planet. True courage comes in enduring . . . and believing in oneself."[3] McNair became the second African American in space when he flew aboard the *Challenger* in 1984. During that mission, he operated the robotic arm used to move payloads in space.

Payload Specialists

Payload specialists are astronauts who carry out experiments on a flight. Perhaps the most excited crew member on *Challenger* was forty-one-year-old Gregory B. Jarvis. He had been scheduled for two earlier flights. He lost his place both times to members of Congress. Jarvis was married to Marcia Jarboe. He worked for the Hughes Aircraft Company and had a master's degree in electrical engineering. He had won his spot after competing against six hundred other employees. His main duty on *Challenger* would be to study liquids in microgravity. Like the other astronauts, Jarvis was not afraid of the dangers of spaceflight. "For any contingency, they know what to do," he said. "So I feel very, very comfortable. I'm excited, but not nervous."[4]

Thirty-six-year-old Sharon Christa McAuliffe taught in a New Hampshire high school. Her husband, Steven, was her high school sweetheart.[5] They had two children. McAuliffe liked classical music but preferred the Beatles.[6] She won her spot on the crew over thousands of teacher applicants. As a young girl, she was excited over the *Apollo* moon landings. When she was seven, she had asked why a monkey had gone into space instead of her.[7]

In 1984, McAuliffe learned about NASA's efforts to find "one of America's finest: a teacher."[8] She and the other applicants underwent

Challenger flight crew members Ronald McNair (left), Gregory Jarvis (center), and Christa McAuliffe participate in a training exercise. Jarvis, who had been scheduled for two earlier missions, was finally getting his opportunity to go into space.

One of Christa McAuliffe's jobs during the mission would be to demonstrate and to explain the effects of microgravity to students watching on television. In this photo, McAuliffe receives a preview of microgravity during a special flight aboard **NASA**'s "zero gravity" aircraft as part of her training.

physical and psychological tests similar to those given to astronauts. In July, McAuliffe was selected to be the first teacher in space.

She wrote on her astronaut application, "I watched the Space Age being born and I would like to participate."[9] Now she would get her chance. McAuliffe had two jobs to do. The first was to demonstrate and to explain to the children the effects of microgravity (a free fall in orbit). She would do this via television from the shuttle.[10] The second was to videotape six science experiments. NASA would distribute these to schools around the country after the flight.[11]

McAuliffe was popular with the media, and the Teacher in Space Program earned positive publicity. Dick Scobee, the mission commander, told her, "You know, shuttle missions are taken for granted these days," he said, "but this one is unique. No matter what happens, this mission will always be remembered as the teacher-in-space mission, and you should be proud of that. We're all proud of that."[12] The tragic death of McAuliffe and the crew forced NASA to reacknowledge the dangers of spaceflight and to make safety changes.

President Ronald Reagan said after the accident, "We remember Christa McAuliffe, who captured the imagination of the entire nation, inspiring us with her pluck, her restless spirit of discovery; a teacher, not just to her students, but to an entire people, instilling us all with the excitement of this journey we ride into the future."[13]

The country was saddened by the accident. People wanted to know why seven brave, young, and intelligent men and women had died. They wanted those answers quickly.

Fragments of the space shuttle tumbling against a background of fire, smoke, and vaporized fuel can be seen in this photo taken about seventy-six seconds into the launch. The left solid rocket booster is seen still thrusting upward. After the disastrous explosion, President Ronald Reagan appointed a special commission to investigate the accident.

CHAPTER 4

Anatomy of the Accident

President Ronald Reagan appointed a special commission to find the cause of the accident. Among its members were General Charles Yeager, the first pilot to break the sound barrier, and Professor Neil Armstrong, the first person to walk on the moon. Dr. Sally Ride stopped training for what would have been her third spaceflight to join the commission.

Presidential Commission on the *Challenger* Accident

The commission became known as the Rogers Commission, named after its chairperson, William P. Rogers. A former U.S. attorney general and secretary of state, Rogers was known for his fairness. The Rogers Commission was ordered to investigate every phase of the doomed mission and to find the cause of the explosion. It would also make recommendations to prevent it from happening again. However, any findings made would have to be backed up with physical proof. This meant examining the debris recovered from the ocean.

Recovery crews had brought up tons of wreckage. The larger pieces included parts of the shuttle and the external fuel tank. They recovered about half the total vehicle, including both solid rocket boosters.[1] The wreckage was taken to a hangar at Cape Canaveral. There it was laid out on a grid and fitted back together wherever possible. Divers also found the flight recorders. Clues as to what went wrong were found on these recorders.

Important Clues

One important clue was a hole burned in part of the right solid rocket booster. While the investigators continued to look at the wreckage, the videotapes of the launch revealed solid clues. The team examined every frame of film and every frame of videotape. They found that less than half a second after ignition, there were puffs of black smoke coming from a joint on the right solid rocket booster. As the rocket rose, it left behind puffs of smoke. A fresh puff could then be seen near the joint.[2] Eight puffs of smoke appeared within two seconds. The smoke hinted that there might be a tiny gap between two sections of the booster.

Something was burning that should not have been burning. The two boosters each were made of eleven cylinders, with walls about one-quarter-inch (.64-centimeter) thick. Tongue-and-groove joints and steel pins connected them to each other. Heat-resistant putty and a pair

Search-and-recovery teams located this joint from the right-hand side of the solid rocket booster, which had traces of O-ring seal tracks. The O-ring failure caused a hole to burn in the right solid rocket booster.

of synthetic rubber O-rings sealed the joints. The O-ring's purpose was to seal the joints and to prevent hot gases from escaping.[3]

The black color of the smoke suggested that the rubber O-rings were being burned away by the rocket's normal exhaust gases. The tape showed the smoke spreading across the booster, and then it was gone. No one saw this smoke during the launch. The commission looked at films of earlier launches to see if this smoke was present. It was not.

For almost a minute, the liftoff seemed perfectly normal. Then, from the flight recorder and the videotape, a terrible picture began to emerge.

At 58.7 seconds, the smoke appeared again. At fifty-nine seconds, the greatest aerodynamic stress was on the vehicle. A second later, hot gas could be seen leaking from the right booster. A seal had burned away. The flight computer tried to adjust to make up for the dropping fuel pressure in the booster. Seconds later, the computers show there was a problem in the liquid oxygen line. The tape showed where the puffs of smoke had been, and that they were replaced by a small flame. The flame had burned through the thin skin of the booster. It acted like a torch, burning through the bracket holding the external tank. The flame

This photo of the *Challenger* space shuttle taken seconds before the explosion shows a flame and hot gas leaking from the side of the right solid rocket booster. The faulty O-ring caused this dangerous leak that led to the explosion.

caused the bracket attached to the booster to break away. The booster then slammed into the external tank. This tank had a super-explosive mixture of fuel. At seventy-three seconds, there is a flash on the videotape, followed by the sound of an explosion on the flight recorder. Then all sounds and data stop.

An Accident Waiting to Happen

This was an accident, but one that did not have to happen. An engineer at Morton Thiokol, the company that made the rocket boosters, had said, ". . . if we do not take immediate action to dedicate a team to solve the problem, . . . then we stand in jeopardy of losing a flight . . . [and] a catastrophe of the highest order—loss of human life."[4] His words were ignored. He knew that someday an accident could occur.

NASA had known for years that the O-ring seals could fail. Out of the first twenty-four shuttle flights, inspections found fifteen instances where the O-rings had been partially burned away.[5] When NASA began using a new putty seal, the trouble got worse. There was damage to O-rings in eight of nine flights in 1985.[6] NASA never told the astronauts of the danger they faced.

Findings

The commission found both mechanical and human failures caused the accident. They concluded that the failure of an O-ring seal on the right solid rocket booster was the main cause of the explosion. However, why did the O-ring fail? The O-rings had frozen overnight, and, at launch, the temperature of the left solid rocket booster was 33°F (.6°C). The right booster was 19°F (–7.2°C). The lower temperature was caused by the wind blowing off the super-cold external fuel tank.[7] In such cold, the rubber O-rings become stiff and inflexible. This allowed the rocket's hot gas to blow past the seal. A giant nine-hundred-dollar rubber band was responsible for the loss of seven lives.

William P. Rogers, chairman of the Rogers Commission, and astronaut Sally Ride examine a cross section of a solid rocket booster during hearings in Washington, D.C. The Rogers Commission's final findings stated three main causes for the *Challenger* accident: cold weather, poor human judgment, and mechanical failure of a joint seal in the right solid rocket booster.

Morton Thiokol's engineers had been aware of the seal issue. Five months before the accident, they had submitted several design changes to NASA. These changes were expensive. NASA decided to delay the changes until the following year, when they had money in the budget.[8]

The commission also found that management and safety issues inside NASA had contributed to the accident. NASA's quality control staff had decreased by 70 percent since Alan Shepard had walked on the moon in 1971. NASA was under serious pressure to speed up the launch schedule. The nation's reliance on the shuttle as its principal space launch vehicle created enormous stress on NASA to increase the flight rate. Technicians worked as many as eighty hours a week, some for two months straight without a day off, trying to meet the launch schedule for that year.[9] "As the flight rate increased, the . . . safety, reliability, and quality assurance work force was decreasing, which adversely affected mission safety," the commission report said.[10] The cause of the accident was due to cold weather, poor human judgment, and mechanical failure of a joint seal in the right solid rocket booster. This tragic accident had a profound effect on future space shuttle launches at NASA.

From this tragedy came some valuable lessons. However, there would be no more shuttle flights until NASA was sure that this would not happen again.

After the *Challenger* accident and the investigation by the Rogers Commission, NASA created new goals for space shuttle flights. The primary mission would be to carry the people and supplies needed to build a space station. The International Space Station is shown in this photo taken on June 3, 1999.

CHAPTER 5

Aftermath

The space shuttle was grounded for thirty-two months after the *Challenger* accident. The largest program of space exploration in history would be put on hold until the shuttle was safe to fly.

Lessons Learned

President Reagan asked NASA to reevaluate the shuttle's place in the space program. As a result, NASA created new goals for shuttle flights. The shuttle's primary mission would be to carry the people and supplies needed to build a space station. "Rocket technology is risky," said Sally Ride. "Those risks are something that every astronaut has to internally come to grips with and be willing to accept."[1]

NASA changed the policy of civilians flying on the shuttle. Only trained, professional astronauts would fly shuttle missions. Previous civilian crew members included members of Congress and even a prince from Saudi Arabia. There would be no teachers or politicians in space for many years. Senator John Glenn's flight in 1998 was an exception. He had been a trained astronaut.

The Rogers Commission recommended several changes to the space shuttle. The most important change was the redesign of the solid rocket booster joints. The engineers redesigned the O-rings, the O-ring seals, and the joints between the booster sections. First, they replaced the putty with an adhesive that made a tighter seal during launch. They added a third O-ring seal, in case the gases reached the adhesive seal. The engineers did not think this would happen, but they were being cautious. They installed temperature sensors and heaters inside the joints. The heaters would keep the temperature of the O-rings at 75°F (23.9°C) at launch. They performed many tests, and the new design performed perfectly during these tests.[2]

The commission called for a new system to manage the shuttle program. NASA would have to establish a flight schedule that did not create safety issues. They also called for better safety and quality control programs to make sure that all materials and procedures were safe.

Keeping Their Memory Alive

To remember the *Challenger* crew, the crew members' families created the *Challenger* Center for Space Science Education. There are fifty-two sites located in thirty-one states and Washington, D.C. There are also two in Canada and one in the United Kingdom. Their goal is to encourage young people to become interested in science and space travel.

Each center has two rooms. One is a mock-up of the Mission Control room. The other is a space lab. The students role-play as astronauts, mission controllers, and scientists. They solve problems

The *Challenger* memorial plaque in Arlington National Cemetery honors the seven crew members who lost their lives during the accident.

that they may encounter on a real mission. Each student is assigned to one of the eight teams on the crew. Halfway through the mission, the students switch places so everyone has an opportunity to experience both Mission Control and the space lab.[3]

NASA created the Astronaut Memorial at the Kennedy Space Center. It honors astronauts who have lost their lives in space exploration. The *Challenger* astronauts' names are carved on the black granite surface. The Space Shuttle *Challenger* Memorial in Arlington National Cemetery, near the Tomb of the Unknown Soldier, shows the faces of all seven crew members.

After more than two years without a shuttle mission, NASA relaunched its space shuttle program with the *Discovery*. In this photo, *Discovery* lifts off from the launchpad at Kennedy Space Center on September 29, 1988.

He Never Came Back

The families of the astronauts sued the government and the Morton Thiokol company. Unknown sums were paid to each family. Jane Smith said, "No one in big business should be allowed to make a faulty product and profit from it." Life goes on, and the families have moved on, too. Steven McAuliffe went back to work as a lawyer raising his two children. Cheryl Moore McNair works for a foundation for teenage mothers. Marcia Jarvis clears hiking trails near her home in California.

Jane Smith works with her favorite charity, the Virginia Beach Society for the Prevention of Cruelty to Animals. Her dogs, she says, helped her through mourning. She still missed Mike Smith every day: "I waited, and he never came back."[4] She has since remarried.

The debris from *Challenger* was taken to an abandoned launch complex. It was sealed in two eighty-foot-deep missile silos. Debris has washed ashore every so often in the years since the explosion. In December 1996, two pieces of *Challenger* washed up on a beach near the Kennedy Space Center. The pieces were put in the silo where the rest of the shuttle is buried.

Rebirth of the Shuttle Program

On September 29, 1988, *Discovery* launched into the warm, blue Florida sky. The launch was perfect. The O-rings did their job. NASA had learned much from the *Challenger* tragedy. Mission Commander Frederick H. Hauck said, "Today, up here where the blue sky turns to black, we can say at long last, to Dick, Mike, Judy, to Ron and El, and to Christa and to Greg . . . dear friends, we have resumed the journey that we promised to continue for you; . . . your spirit and your dream are still alive in our hearts."[5]

Safety Record

By October 2002, eighty-six shuttle missions had been launched safely since *Challenger*.[6] The attitude of "hurry up and launch" was gone. In June 2002, NASA discovered a small crack within the fuel lines on *Atlantis*. Instead of launching the next flight, NASA inspected all the shuttles. This meant the expensive removal of the shuttle's main engines. There were similar cracks in all the shuttles. NASA grounded all flights until October. The shuttle did not fly until NASA discovered what caused the cracks and how to prevent them in the future.

Tragedy, though, would strike again. On February 1, 2003, the space shuttle *Columbia* exploded as it reentered Earth's atmosphere over the state of Texas. In this case, a piece of insulating foam had fallen off one of the gas tanks and damaged the left wing of the ship during takeoff. The wing was unable to withstand the heat on reentry, and the entire shuttle exploded. Seven astronauts were killed.

Educator in Space

At the time of the *Challenger* accident, President Reagan was hopeful. "There will be more shuttle flights," he said, "and more shuttle crews and, yes, more volunteers, more civilians, more teachers in space."[7] But NASA said there would be no more civilians on shuttle flights. Still, they left open the possibility for a future Teacher in Space Program. It said, "When NASA determines a flight opportunity is available for a space-flight participant, first priority will be given to a 'Teacher in Space'...."[8]

Barbara Morgan served as Christa McAuliffe's backup on the *Challenger* mission. She trained with McAuliffe and the *Challenger* crew. She taught reading and math. When *Challenger* exploded, the Teacher in Space Program ended. Barbara Morgan never gave up her dream of going to space. She returned to her teaching career, but she continued to work with NASA to finish what McAuliffe had set out to accomplish. Each year she took her flight physical. She was waiting for the day that NASA would restart the program.

NASA selected Morgan as its first educator mission specialist, and in April 2002, NASA Administrator Sean O'Keefe said: "The time has come [for] NASA to complete the mission—to send an educator to space to inspire and teach our young people. . . . We will make Barbara's

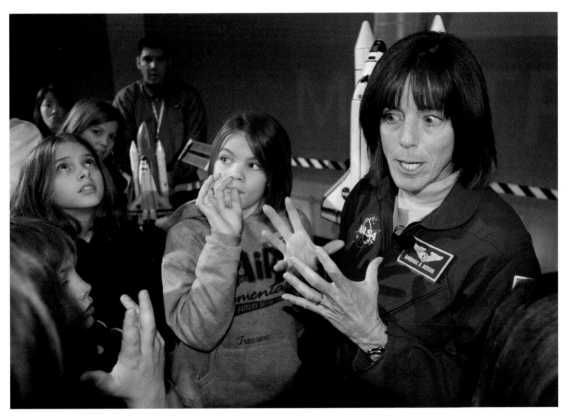

Astronaut Barbara Morgan talks to students about her upcoming mission during "Meet an Astronaut Day" at Space Center Houston on January 19, 2007. Eight months later, Morgan flew into space as part of the crew aboard the space shuttle *Endeavour*. She accomplished the job that Christa McAuliffe had set out to complete twenty-one years earlier.

(Morgan) flight the first in a series of missions in the new Educator in Space program."[9]

Morgan worked in the Mission Control Center as the communicator with shuttle crews. She was scheduled to fly after completion of the core elements of the International Space Station in 2004. However, on February 1, 2003, the explosion of the space shuttle *Columbia* changed those plans. The remaining three space shuttles were grounded indefinitely until investigators could determine the cause of the accident. Then they had to put procedures in place so an explosion like that would not happen again.

It took more than two years before NASA would launch another space shuttle on July 26, 2005. Finally, on August 8, 2007, Barbara Morgan achieved her dream of spaceflight. She served as a mission specialist aboard the space shuttle *Endeavour* during the twenty-second flight to the International Space Station. The *Endeavour* remained in space for twelve days, continuing construction on the space station. In addition to serving as robotic arm operator and transfer coordinator, Morgan participated in educational interviews and experiments via radio to students at space centers in Idaho, Virginia, and Massachusetts.

Morgan finished the job that McAuliffe had set out to achieve. Her mission served as a memorial to McAuliffe and the brave *Challenger* crew. "What happened [with *Challenger*] was horrible," said Morgan, "and you can't ever erase that. But our job as teachers is to help kids reach their potential. *Challenger* reminds us that we should never quit reaching for the stars."[10]

Chapter Notes

Chapter 1. The Final Voyage

1. Robert T. Hohler, *I Touch the Future. . . : The Story of Christa McAuliffe* (New York: Random House, 1986), p. 49.
2. Author witness to launch of shuttle *Columbia*, April 4, 1981.
3. Steve Garber, curator, "Transcript of the *Challenger* Crew Comments From the Operational Recorder," *National Aeronautics and Space Administration*, February 3, 2003, <http://www.hq.nasa.gov/office/pao/History/transcript.html> (October 30, 2002).
4. David Shayler, *Shuttle Challenger* (New York: Prentice Hall Press, 1987), p. 49.

Chapter 2. Launch Background

1. Robert T. Hohler, *I Touch the Future. . . : The Story of Christa McAuliffe* (New York: Random House, 1986), p. 248.
2. Jay Barbree, "Chapter 1: A Chill at the Cape," *MSNBC News*, 2003, <http://www.msnbc.com/news/510544.asp> (October 30, 2002).
3. Richard Lewis, *Challenger: The Final Voyage* (New York: Columbia University Press, 1988), p. 131.
4. Barbree, "A Chill at the Cape."
5. Ed Magnuson, "They Slipped the Surly Bonds of Earth to Touch the Face of God," *Time*, February 10, 1986, p. 26.
6. Kay Grinter, curator, "Space Shuttle TAL Sites," *John F. Kennedy Space Center*, May 15, 2001, <http://www-pao.ksc.nasa.gov/kscpao/nasafact/tal.htm#top> (October 30, 2002).
7. Magnuson, p. 26.
8. Lewis, p. 3.
9. Tommy W. Holloway, "Mission Planning and Operation Team Report," *Report of the Presidential Commission on the Space Shuttle Challenger Accident, May 1986,* <http://history.nasa.gov/rogersrep/v2appj.htm> (October 30, 2002).
10. David Shayler, *Shuttle Challenger* (New York: Prentice Hall Press, 1987), p. 49.
11. Joseph P. Kerwin, "Letter to Admiral Richard H. Truly," *National Aeronautics and Space Administration*, July 28, 1986, <http://www.hq.nasa.gov/office/pao/History/kerwin.html> (October 30, 2002).
12. Magnuson, p. 25.

13. Claudia Glenn Dowling, "Ten Years Ago, Seven Brave Americans Died as They Reached for the Stars," *Life*, February 1996, p. 39.

14. Lewis, p. 22.

15. Claudia Glenn Dowling, "From the February 1996 issue of *Life*," *The Mission Continues*, n.d., <http://www.life.com/Life/space/challenger/challenger04.html> (October 30, 2002).

16. Malcolm McConnell, *Challenger: A Major Malfunction* (Garden City, N.Y.: Doubleday & Company, Inc., 1987), p. 247.

17. Ronald Reagan, "The White House, January 28, 1986," *Reagan's Remarks*, <http://www.chron.com/content/interactive/special/challenger/docs/reagan.html> (October 30, 2002).

18. Kerwin, "Letter to Admiral Richard H. Truly."

19. Ibid.

20. Ibid.

Chapter 3. The Seven Heroes

1. Paul Gray, "Seven Who Flew for All of Us," *Time*, February 10, 1986, p. 33.

2. Ibid.

3. Ibid., p. 34.

4. Ibid., p. 35.

5. Robert T. Hohler, *I Touch the Future. . . : The Story of Christa McAuliffe* (New York: Random House, 1986), p. 5.

6. Ibid.

7. Ibid., p. 55.

8. Ibid., p. 97.

9. Ibid., p. 64.

10. Richard Lewis, *Challenger: The Final Voyage* (New York: Columbia University Press, 1988), p. 1.

11. Hohler, p. 170.

12. Ibid., p. 150.

13. Ronald Reagan, "A President's Eulogy," 1st Anniversary, January 31, 1986, <http://www.chron.com/content/interactive/special/challenger/docs/eulogy.html> (October 30, 2002).

Chapter 4. Anatomy of the Accident

1. Cliff Lethbridge, "The *Challenger* Legacy," *Spaceline*, 2000, <http://www.spaceline.org/challenger.html#3> (October 30, 2002).

2. Tommy W. Holloway, "Mission Planning and Operation Team Report," *Report of the*

Presidential Commission on the Space Shuttle Challenger Accident, May 1986, <http://history .nasa.gov/rogersrep/v1ch3.htm> (October 30, 2002).

3. Richard Lewis, *Challenger: The Final Voyage* (New York: Columbia University Press, 1988), p. 63.

4. Holloway, "Mission Planning and Operation Team Report."

5. Lewis, p. 76.

6. Ibid.

7. Ibid., p. 126.

8. Wayne Biddle, "What Destroyed *Challenger*?" *Discover,* April 1986, p. 46.

9. Robert T. Hohler, *I Touch the Future. . . : The Story of Christa McAuliffe* (New York: Random House, 1986), p. 235.

10. Holloway, "Mission Planning and Operation Team Report."

Chapter 5. Aftermath

1. Laura S. Woodmansee, *Women Astronauts* (Ontario, Canada: Apogee Books, 2002), p. 44.

2. "The *Challenger* Accident: An Analysis of the Mechanical and Administrative Causes of the Accident and the Redesign Process That Followed," *Mechanical Redesign,* n.d., <http:// www.me.utexas.edu/~uer/challenger/chall4.html#oringerosion> (October 30, 2002).

3. "*Challenger* Learning Centers," *Challenger* Center for Space Science Education, 2003, <http://www.challenger.org/clc/clc_tell_set.htm> (October 30, 2002).

4. Claudia Glenn Dowling, "From the February 1996 issue of *Life*," *The Mission Continues,* n.d., <http://www.life.com/Life/space/challenger/challenger05.html> (October 30, 2002).

5. "MCC Status Reports," *Spacelink,* 1988, <http://spacelink.nasa.gov/NASA.Projects/ Human.Exploration.and.Development.of.Space/Human.Space.Flight/Shuttle/Shuttle .Missions/Flight.026.STS-26/MCC.Status.Reports> (October 30, 2002).

6. Jim Dumoulin, "NASA Space Shuttle Launches," *Space Shuttle Launches,* February 1, 2003, <http://science.ksc.nasa.gov/shuttle/missions/> (October 30, 2002).

7. Dowling, "From the February 1996 issue of *Life*."

8. "Aeronautics and Space," Code of Federal Regulations, January 1, 2003, <http:// a257.g.akamaitech.net/7/257/2422/14mar20010800/edocket.acces.../14cfr1214.303 .htm) (September 17, 2003).

9. Bob Jacobs, "Administrator Unveils Future NASA Vision and a Renewed Journey of Learning," *NASA,* <ftp://ftp.hq.nasa.gov/pub/pao/pressrel/2002/02-066.txt> (October 30, 2002).

10. Dowling, "From the February 1996 issue of *Life*."

Glossary

downlink—The radio communication between Mission Control and a spacecraft.

external fuel tank—The large tank filled with liquid fuel that feeds the shuttle orbiter's main engines.

microgravity—A condition in space in which only minuscule forces are experienced, or a virtual absence of gravity.

Mission Control Center—A room filled with computers where flight controllers monitor spaceflights.

mission specialists—Astronauts who operate the mechanical systems on the space shuttle.

O-ring—The large rubber ring used to seal sections of the solid rocket boosters together.

payload specialists—Astronauts who conduct experiments on a spaceflight.

reentry—The return of a spacecraft through Earth's atmosphere.

solid rocket booster—A rocket that uses explosive powders for fuel.

space shuttle—The reusable U.S. space transportation system that carries astronauts, satellites, and experimental scientific equipment into Earth orbit.

Further Reading

Books

Caper, William. *The Challenger Space Shuttle Explosion*. New York: Bearport, 2007.

Gogerly, Liz. *The Challenger, 1986: A Space Shuttle Explodes After Lift-off*. Chicago: Raintree, 2006.

McNeese, Tim. *The Challenger Disaster*. New York: Children's Press, 2003.

Woods, Michael, and Mary B. Woods. *Space Disasters*. Minneapolis, Minn.: Lerner Publishing Group, 2008.

Internet Addresses

Challenger Center for Space Science Education
<http://www.challenger.org/>

NASA: STS-51L—*Challenger* Mission Profile
<http://www.nasa.gov/mission_pages/shuttle/shuttlemissions/archives/sts-51L.html>

NASA: Space Shuttle
<http://www.nasa.gov/mission_pages/shuttle/main/index.html>

Index

A

Apollo, 14, 23
Armstrong, Neil, 27
Astronaut Memorial, 37
Atlantis, 40

C

Challenger
  burial of, 39
  crew compartment, 17–18
  explosion, 7–9
  flight crew, 19–21
  history of, 11
  launch, 5–6
  launch delays, 11–13
  liftoff, 6
  mission specialists, 21–22
  payload specialists, 22–25
  rocket ignition, 6, 13–14
Challenger Center for Space
  Science Education, 36–37
Columbia, 9, 40, 42

D

Discovery, 21, 39

E

Endeavour, 42
explosion
  cause of, 31–33
  cause of deaths, 18
  crew recovery, 16–18
  described, 7–9, 14
  investigation of, 27–31

public reaction to,
  14–16, 25

G

Glenn, John, 35

I

International Space Station,
  42

J

Jarvis, Gregory B., 6, 22

L

lawsuits, 38

M

McAuliffe, Christa, 5, 7, 9,
  14, 22–25, 40–41, 42
McNair, Ronald E., 6, 21–22
Morgan, Barbara, 40–42
Morton Thiokol, 31, 33, 38

N

NASA
  civilians in space, 35,
  40–42
  on crew deaths, 18
  decision to launch, 12
  memorials, 37
  policy changes by, 35,
  39–40
  public relations by, 16, 25
  safety issues, 11, 33, 36

withholding of
  information by, 31

O

Onizuka, Ellison S., 6, 21
O-rings, 12, 13, 29, 31–32,
  36, 39

R

Reagan, Ronald, 16–17, 25,
  35, 40
Resnik, Judith A., 6, 21
Ride, Sally, 21, 27, 35
rocket boosters, 6, 11–14,
  28–31, 36
Rogers, William P., 27
Rogers Commission,
  27–28, 36

S

Scobee, Francis "Dick," 6, 7,
  19–20
Smith, Michael J., 6, 7, 15,
  20–21, 25
Space Shuttle Challenger
  Memorial, 37

T

Teacher in Space Program,
  5, 25, 40

Y

Yeager, Charles, 27